verpool Everyman & Playhouse theatres
esent the world premiere of

CW01499718

TAKEAWAY

BY NATHAN POWELL

rst performed on 26 April 2025
the Everyman theatre, Liverpool

CAST

ADI ALFA
BROWNING

BILL CAPLE
RICHARD

PHINA ORUCHE
CAROL

WAYNE ROLLINS
CHEF

BENE SEBUYANGE
SHELLY

WITH THE VOICES OF:
ELISE DONNELLY
CHARLIE SEALEY
SHARON WALKER

WITH THANKS TO
RAGGAS

COMPANY

WRITER
NATHAN POWELL

DIRECTOR
AMANDA HUXTABLE

SET & COSTUME DESIGNER
GEORGIA WILMOT

LIGHTING DESIGNER
LAURA HOWARD

SOUND DESIGNER
ERNEST ACQUAH

YEP TRAINEE ASSISTANT DIRECTOR
SCARLET (RED) ROBINSON-STANLEY

DIALECT COACH
CLAUDETTE WILLIAMS

PRODUCER
MICHELLE CAILLEUX

ASSISTANT PRODUCER
ZOE WALKER

PRODUCTION MANAGER
DAN FRANKLIN

ASSISTANT PRODUCTION MANAGER
DIEGO GUTIÉRREZ CÓRDOBA

COMPANY MANAGER
SARAH LEWIS

STAGE MANAGER
KATE ECCLES

DEPUTY STAGE MANAGER
SAF HORROCKS

ASSISTANT STAGE MANAGER
KAILA SHARPLES

ASSISTANT STAGE MANAGER
TILLY FORSTER

BOOK COVER
BETH LEWIS-CLAREY

LX PROGRAMMER
JACK WOODS

LX SUPPORT
ANDY WEBSTER, JACK HIGHAM, JENNIFER CHISLETT

LX OPERATOR
JENNIFER CHISLETT

SENIOR SOUND TECHNICIAN
IAN DAVIES

SENIOR STAGE TECHNICIAN
MIKE CANTLEY

STAGE SHOW CREW
JACK WOODS, MIKE CANTLEY, JENNIFER CHISLETT, OLLY MORRIS

STAGE FIT-UP CREW
**DAVE MCGOVERN, KEITH HOLT, OLLY MORRIS,
RHYS LOCKHART, HARRY SOUTH**

COSTUME SUPERVISOR
CATE MACKIE

SET CONSTRUCTION AND SCENIC ART
LIVERPOOL SCENIC

ADDITIONAL SCENIC ART
ABBIE JONES

BRITISH SIGN LANGUAGE PERFORMANCE
SUMAYYA SI TAYEB

AUDIO DESCRIBED PERFORMANCE
FAITH AGBA FOR MIND'S EYE

CAPTIONED PERFORMANCE
KAY GEORGE

COVER PHOTOGRAPH
KERRY SPICER

LIPA PLACEMENT
ALEX JONES

ADI ALFA | BROWNING

Adi is a multi award-winning actress with over 15 years experience across screen, stage, and voice. Originally from Liverpool and now based in the South, she has carved out a dynamic and diverse career in the arts. She has worked as an actress globally including America, Europe and the Caribbean. Adi is the founder of Media Worx Films, a multi award-winning production company known for producing bold, impactful content and championing underrepresented voices. Their next project has been shortlisted for the BFI Early Development Fund

TV & Film credits include: Liverpool-based Channel 4 drama *The Gathering*, Netflix's *The Intent*, and the recently released *Traces*. Committed to representation and storytelling, Adi is developing several original TV series she will also star in—bringing to life narratives that centre brown and Black Liverpudlian voices.

Theatre credits & Voice Acting credits include:
BAFTA-winning game *Disco Elysium*; the BAFTA-nominated *The Falconeer* and *The Ballerina* (Vault)

BILL CAPLE | RICHARD

Bill trained at the Bristol Old Vic Theatre school.

TV & Film credits include: *The Responder*; *Buckingham Murders*; *Doctors*; *Outlander* and *Sugarland*.

Theatre credits include: *Dear England* (National Theatre

PHINA ORUCHE | CAROL

Phina began her career as a fashion model in London, before emigrating to New York. She trained at the renowned Actors Studio in Los Angeles.

Theatre credits include: *Identity Crisis* (her one woman show which opened at the Edinburgh Fringe and has since played in London, Bristol, Manchester, NYC and Shakespeare North).

UK TV & Film credits include: *Unforgiven; Magpie Murders; Anthony; Moving On; Taken Down; Hollyoaks; Little Miss Jocelyn* and *Footballers Wives.*

US TV & Film credits include: *The Pretender; VIP; Nash Bridges; Nip/Tuck; Charmed; Buffy The Vampire Slayer; Diagnosis Murder* and *NYPD Blue.*

Other credits include: Phina has also been a regular panellist on entertainment and talk shows such as The Wright Stuff and has produced and hosted her own radio show for BBC Radio Merseyside. She is also a published writer, with the books *Jacopo Jacopo Football Star* and *Jacopo Jacopo on Lockdown* which both came out in 2020 on Amazon. Currently she is working on her new play writing and rehearsing to perform *Cancel Culture.*

WAYNE ROLLINS | CHEF

Making his Liverpool debut, Wayne is an all-round entertainer whose career spans the globe over the decades in everything from *Rastamouse* Live to *Gangster Kittens.* He also is a professional DJ as well as an actor.

Theatre credits include: Pantomime residence as Dame Dibbi the Dancehall Queen, *Young Gifted and Phat and Why Me?* (Broadway Theatre, Catford); *Nine Night* (Leeds Playhouse); *Sucker Punch* (Curve Leicester); *Josie and the Multicoloured Weave* (The Open Door Theatre); *Real Housewives of Brixton, Scrooge* and his solo show, *Will the Real Wayne Rollins Stand Up* (Hackney Empire).

Other project credits include: *Ted Lasso* (season two), commercials for Experian with Marcus Brigstocke and a memorable role opposite Dizzee Rascal in his *Money Right* video.

BENE SEBUYANGE | SHELLY

Bene is a Northwest-based actor and spoken word artist. She is a two-time slam champion with The Poet Society and continues to develop her work across theatre and spoken word.

Theatre credits include: *Smiles* (Shakespeare North Playhouse, Unity Theatre, and community spaces).

Other stage work feature performances at: Soho Theatre and Theatre503, alongside spoken word appearances nationwide, including at the Royal Festival

THAN POWELL | WRITER

ithan is the Creative Director of the Liverpool Everyman & Playhouse theatres.

eviously Artistic Director of the National Student Drama Festival (NSDF), Nathan has
ampioned emerging talent and forged groundbreaking partnerships, showcasing
me of the most exciting new work from across the country. He was the Creative
oducer and Associate Artist for 20 Stories High (an Associate Company of the theatres)
d is co-founder of New Step Theatre with writer Joe Ward Munrow (their production
DOGS was a sellout in the Playhouse Studio in 2022).

a director his recent credits include: *Alice in Wonderland* (Shakespeare North
ayhouse); *The Mountaintop* (Leicester Curve and UK Tour); *Sucker Punch* (Queens
eatre Hornchurch in association with the National Theatre) and *A Play for the Living in
e Time of Extinction* (Headlong and The Barbican in association with Shakespeare
rth).

IANDA HUXTABLE | DIRECTOR

nanda has over 25 years of experience in the creative industries. She is a highly
garded Theatre Director and has worked across the UK and Internationally.
esenting productions around the world including at the biannual National Black
eatre Festival in the USA and as part of the British Council in Sierra Leone, supporting
iters with script development for screen and live work for British Council Venezuela.
nanda is former co-director of Vanitas Arts and has recently completed her role as co
rector of GeoStories.

nen it comes to story, Amanda has actively worked for the diversification of the
ltural sector in the United Kingdom all her professional life and has been an invited
est speaker at The University of Manchester Advanced Directing, The University of
eds MA Writers and The Arden School of Theatre MA Directors.

a director her recent credits include: *Nine Night* and *Unknown* (Leeds Playhouse);
rsons of Interests Audio Drama Series, *Trumpet, I leave you love* and *Ladies of
uations* (Vanitas Arts); *Everything I Own* and *Abigail's Party* (Hull Truck Theatre);
ead and Roses and *The Engagement Party* (Oldham Coliseum); *Wondr* (Metta
eatre, Edinburgh Festival); *Bag Lady* (Hidden Gems); *Hilda and the Northern
werhouse* (Kate Hainsworth) and *Just an Ordinary Lawyer?* (Tayo Aluko & Friends).

her credits include: Chair of the Board for Reggae Jazz Contemporary Dance, Leeds
d is a Committee Member for Huddersfield Literary Festival. Recently she has
come a BAFTA Connect Member.

GEORGIA WILMOT | SET & COSTUME DESIGNER

Georgia trained in Interior Design at Liverpool John Moores University before moving in to Theatre Production and Costume Design. In 2024 Georgia was thrilled to be nominated for a Black British Theatre Award in the Theatre Design (body of work) category.

As a set & costume designer credits include: *Conversations After Sex* (Park Theatre); *Cross the Line* (Lyric Hammersmith); *Communion, The End Red Pitch, Elephant, Clutch, Invisible, The Kola Nut Does Not Speak English, BACK UP!, The Route* and *Project* (Bush Theatre); *Before I Go* (Brixton House); *Red Pitch* (Soho Place); *This Is A Love Story* (Birmingham Hippodrome); *Proof, Three Sisters, Chaos* and *Animal Farm* (St Marys University Summer Festival Production); *The Wrong Reindeer* (Oldham Theatre Workshop); *The Time Has Come* (The Playground Theatre); *Invisible* (59E59 Theatre); *Covered* (New Heritage Theatre at Paddington Arts Centre); *I knew you* (Birmingham Repertory Theatre) and *Days Of Significance* (Questors Theatre).

Writing & illustration credits include: *The Adventures Of* (Book 1, series of children's books, Illustrator); *My Trauma, My Healing* (Instagram, Illustrator); *Life, Lemons and Melons* (Illustrator) and *The Tiger in the Trilby* (Author and Illustrator).

Television, Advertising & Social Media credits include: *Monroe* (ITV -costume trainee) and Superdrug's YouTube channel Christmas campaign 2017

LAURA HOWARD | LIGHTING DESIGNER

Credits for the Everyman & Playhouse: *The Lieutenant of Inishmore* and *The Legend of Ned Ludd* (Liverpool Everyman).

Theatre credits include: *The Habits* (Hampstead Theatre); *Mr Snow* (Leeds Playhouse); *Bangers* (Arcola); *The Good John Proctor* (Jermyn Street Theatre); *Lavender, Hyacinth, Violet, Yew, This Might Not Be It, Invisible, Elephant, Clutch* and *The Kola Nut Does Not Speak English* (Bush Theatre); *Work It Out* (HOME, Manchester); *The Beach House* (Park 90; *Faun* (UK Tour, Cardboard Citizens); *Santi & Naz, Splintered, curious, Juniper & Jules* and *Dismissed* (Soho Theatre); *Salty Irina* (Paines Plough Roundabout at Summerhall); *Brassic Fm* (Gate Theatre); *Black Is...*(New Diorama); *Snow Queen* (Polka Theatre); *Cells Out* (Camden People's Theatre, Glasshouse Theatre); *Moreno* (Theater 503); *I Hate It Here* (Camden People's Theatre & Omnibus Theatre, Sweet Beef Theatre); *Dead Air* (Riverside Studios, Stockroom); *Exodus* (National Theatre of Scotland, Scottish Tour) and *Manorism* (Southbank Centre).

NEST ACQUAH | SOUND DESIGNER

nest is the Creative Engagement Co-ordinator at the Stephen Joseph Theatre and
orks as a freelance Sound Designer. He studied Creative Music Technology at the
iversity of Hull, Scarborough Campus.

eatre credits include: *Alice in Wonderland, The Wind in The Willows* and *A Christmas
arol* (Shakespeare North Playhouse: Sound Designer); *Show and Tell* (SJT: Associate
und Designer); *Road* (YMCA/Coventry University: Sound Designer): *DNA, Collected
'imm Tales, Thor's Great Big Adventure, These Majestic Creatures, Coventry University
owcase, Game Over, The Giant Who Had It All* (And Then Lost It), *Children of Killers,
e Swing of Things, My Own Show, Grimm Tales and Jim of the Garden* (SJT: Sound
esigner); *Build A Rocket* (2023 Edinburgh Festival and tour: Sound Designer); *Constant
ompanions* (SJT: Associate Sound Designer); *Be Gay Do Crime* (Shakespeare North
ayhouse/Transcend Theatre R&D: Musical Director); *Sammy The Shoemaker's
possible Day, The Sad Club, The Adventures of Aluki and Nanuk and Thumbelina* (SJT:
und Designer/Stage Manager); *Jack and the Beanstalk* (Eastfield Youth Theatre:
rector/Sound Designer); *Antigone* (YMCA/Coventry University: Sound Designer);
arky and the Mad-dogs Magical Musical Tour* (Actor-Musician/Sound Designer); *Billy
ite Sally By the Sea* (SJT: Sound Designer/Composer/Stage Manager) and *Colin the
aveman Invents the Wheel* (SJT: Actor/Sound Designer/Composer).

ARLET (RED) ROBINSON-STANLEY | YEP TRAINEE ASSISTANT DIRECTOR

d Robinson-Stanley is an experienced actor, writer and director. From the ages of
18, she was a member of Derby Youth Theatre and went on to be a member of The
levision Workshop in Nottingham where she trained to be a professional screen actor.
d is currently an English and Film Studies student at the University of Liverpool and
keaway is Red's first role as a Trainee Assistant Director on a professional theatre
oduction.

eatre credits include: *You, Door* and multiple other productions (Derby Youth
eatre). This year Red will debut her one woman show *WHITE* at the Edinburgh Fringe
stival.

credits include: *Without Sin* (ITV) and a FIFA mental health awareness campaign.

LIVERPOOL EVERYMAN & PLAYHOUSE

Liverpool's theatres, Sparking Creativity and Nurturing Talent

Rooted in Liverpool's spirit, the Everyman & Playhouse are a creative powerhouse with national and international impact, driven by a passion for theatre, the city, and the belief that theatre can entertain, inspire and fuel positive social change.

With two distinctive venues, each rich in history, they offer unforgettable experiences that captivate the imagination and ignite curiosity. Producing local stories with national impact, the champion emerging talent, innovative storytelling and breathe new life into the classics. Liverpool Everyman & Playhouse want to be the most exciting places to experience and create theatre

A registered charity (1081229), the theatres acknowledge the continued support of Arts Council England and Liverpool City Council, and their audiences, donors, patrons and partners.

For audiences, artists, and communities alike, Liverpool Everyman & Playhouse are places of wonder, magic, and extraordinary moments waiting for you to enjoy.

everymanplayhouse.com

 @livEveryPlay /everymanplayhouse

R THE EVERYMAN & PLAYHOUSE

cutive Team
Da Vanzo Chief Executive
an Powell Creative Director
homas Finance Director

stic Team
elle Cailleux Producer
no Fowler New Works Associate
e Mavrommatis Artistic Administrator
e Nelson Head of Producing & Programming
Walker Assistant Producer

duction Team
ael Cantley Senior Technician (Stage)
fer Chislett Technician (Multi-skilled)
e Davies Senior Technician (Lighting)
avies Senior Technician (Sound & AV)
Franklin Head of Production
o Gutiérrez Córdoba Assistant Production Manager
Higham Technician (Multi-skilled)
Lewis-Clarey Production Coordinator
h Lewis Company Manager
Mackie Head of Costume
rt Newman Senior Technician (Sound & AV)
fer Tallon-Cahill Technical Manager
Webster Senior Technician (Lighting)
Wood Technician (Multi-skilled)

ng People & Community
a Callaghan Community & Education Manager
Hall Young People's Advocate
ey Lindley-Thornhill Head of Young People & Community
n Sing Young People & Community Technical Manager
n Webster Young People & Community Producer

erations & Administration
Adlard Head of Administration
n Griffiths Operations Manager
h Kelly Executive Assistant
ey Wilson HR Officer

ates
ny Delamere Facilities Technician
han Doherty Cleaning & Facilities Team
Miguel Fernandez Facilities Assistant
Fisher Cleaning Team
eeman IT Officer
Manson Cleaning Team
nic Phillips Head of Estates
edden Cleaning Team
ey Warren Cleaning Team
tal Warren Cleaning Team
ey Watts Cleaning Team

Audience Experience
Leah Abbott Audience Experience Coordinator
(Box Office & Stage Door)
Abbie Bates Audience Experience Manager
(Resources)
Brendan Douglas Head of Audience Experience
James Eadan Duty Manager
(Hospitality & Events)
George Fragakis Audience Experience Duty Manager
(Box Office & Stage Door)
Rory Gillan Duty Manager
Jules Goddard Audience Experience Duty Manager
(Box Office & Stage Door)
Melissa James Duty Manager
(Front of House)
Andrew King Box Office & Stage Door Manager
Jason Kelly Audience Experience Assistant
(Box Office & Stage Door)
Mike Lancaster Audience Experience Manager
(Bars & Events)
Kathy Lawrence Audience Experience Assistant
(Box Office & Stage Door)
Gary Lun Audience Experience Assistant
(Box Office & Stage Door)
Hermione Marshall Audience Experience Assistant
(Box Office & Stage Door)
Jack Molloy Duty Manager
Julia Molteberg Duty Manager
(Hospitality & Events)
Ian Nenna Audience Experience Assistant
(Box Office & Stage Door)
Gillian Parry Audience Experience Assistant
(Box Office & Stage Door)
Harry Sargent Audience Experience Assistant
(Box Office & Stage Door)
Raquel Teixeira Duty Manager
Leah Wallace Audience Experience Duty Manager
(Box Office & Stage Door)
Hywell Wilkie Duty Manager
(Hospitality & Events)

Commercial
Elise Donnelly Catering Manager
Rachel Elliott-Newton Venue & Events Planner Manager
Ruth O'Neill Head of Commercial Development

Finance
Stephen Dickson Finance Manager
Rose Hart Finance Assistant
Nicola Jackson Finance Officer

Marketing & Fundraising
Eleanor Bartley Graphic Design Officer
Olivia Carroll Marketing Officer
Rosalind Gordon Fundraising Manager
Ellie Luke Marketing Assistant
Gemma Murrell Marketing Manager
Sarah Ogle Marketing & Communications Director
Chun-Mei Wang Communications Officer

Thanks to all our Audience Experience Team

THANK YOU

Liverpool Everyman & Playhouse are a registered charity (1081229) and gratefully acknowledge the support of our funders, donors, patrons, partners and audiences.

For their ongoing financial support, we would like to thank

The Austin and Hope Pilkington Trust, Backstage Trust, The Foyle Foundation, Garfield Weston Foundation, Idlewild Trust, The Ken Dodd Foundation

Our HE Partner
Edge Hill University

Our Business members & sponsors
Benson Signs, Bruntwood, Duncan Sheard Glass, Hope Street Hotel, Knowsley Chamber of Commerce, Liverpool Growth Platform, Liverpool and Sefton Chamber of Commerce, Professional Liverpool, Rathbone Investment Management, Wirral Chamber of Commerce, Wrightsure Insurance Group

Our Alumni supporters
Jim Broadbent, Matthew Kelly, Sir Ian McKellen, David Morrissey, Bill Nighy, Eddie Redmayne, Willy Russell, Julie Walters

Our Patrons
Steve and Lorraine Groves, Alan Sprince, Lara and Richie Pearn, John and Mary Belcher, Robin Bloxsidge and Nick Riddle, John Birkenhead, Andrea Nixon and Dan StinsonPaul Herbert, Cath and Phil Kightley

Those who have left a Legacy or gave an In Memory gift
Dorothy Smellie, Anni Parker & Brian Barry, lovers and supporters of theatre, Malcolm & Roger Frood in memory of Graham & Joan Frood, Michael Key, Fanchon Frolich, The Dunham Family in loving memory of Matthew Dunham, Board Member and friend

Those who give monthly or annually for their continued support and to everyone who supported the new Everyman Ev4Ev campaign, our Young Everyman and Playhouse appeal in 2022/23, and our Everyone Starts Somewhere campaign in 2024/25.

TAKEAWAY

Nathan Powell

For Jennifer and Lennox

The love you've both put into the world will live forever

Acknowledgements

This play is a true labour of love, that has sat with me for ten years now. It has seen me through various changes in life, career and outlook on the world. The consistent throughout that time has been my family who have supported me immeasurably over this past decade, and whose humour and love have inspired this play. Mum, Merx, Gareth, Aunty Cec, Aunty Carmen, Erin, Beth, Dave, Nia, Asa, Sarai and Remi. Thank you for holding me down.

Thank you to the wonderful team I have joined at the Everyman and Playhouse for your trust in me as an artist. Thank you, Amanda, for your stewardship of this work, and the pride you have instilled in me. Thank you, Barbara and Miriam, for your guidance, truth and care. Thank you, Floriana and Bridie, for being the first people to read *Takeaway* and believe in it. Thank you, Barrington, for pushing me to think beyond boundaries. Thank you, Joe, Luke, Keith, Julia and Brodie, for your constant support and friendship.

Thank you, Zadie, Teilo and Eti for reminding me that it's just never that deep!

And most importantly thank you Lucy, for making everything I do possible. The facilitator of dreams.

N.P.

Characters

CAROL, *mother and owner of the takeaway shop Hyltons.*
  Has a powerful presence
SHELLY, *the youngest daughter. Recently returned from*
  London
BROWNING, *the eldest daughter. Open and free. Unassuming.*
  Very emotionally intelligent
CHEF, *the restaurant's cook. Has a deep care for the family, is*
  almost part of it. Relaxed and calming
RICHARD, *Shelly's boyfriend. Works as a housing officer. Grew*
  up in Toxteth, still slightly uncomfortable around family
TC, *DJ*
CEE, *DJ*
NEWS REPORTER
PRESENTER

Notes on the Text

A forward slash (/) indicates overlapping text.

An em-dash (—) indicates a hard or loaded silence.

*This text went to press before the end of rehearsals and so may
differ slightly from the play as performed.*

ACT ONE

Scene One

Day one.

We are in a radio station. Two DJs are behind some decks for their morning show.

TC. Good morning, good morning, you're back with DJ True Colours and Mista Cee, that was the new Buju, dropped this week, let us know what you think.

CEE. Yes yes, drop us a text on zero-one-eight-seven-four or tweet us at Late Breakfast, that's – (*Spelled out.*) @L8 BREAKFAST and give us your thoughts.

We wanna know how your weekend has been, it has now been confirmed that this is the hottest summer in the UK on record, we want to know how you've been enjoying it. What did you get up to who did you get under – (*Laughter.*)

TC (*kisses teeth*). Cee, you nah know this is a family show! In more important news, we've been hearing some reports about disturbances in the area; More people have been taking to the streets today to protest the planning approval given to build luxury apartments on the site of the football pitches next to Hyltons takeaway. Several arrests have already been made as small pockets of protesters have clashed with the police.

CEE. We've been here before, people, so please, everyone stay safe out there. In here, we want to keep spreading the love.

TC. Yes, yes, people, it's time to wake up, fellas shake up, ladies lace up. Start your day right and the sun will shine bright, walk with a smile and you'll live a long while, fill the world with laughter and we'll avoid disaster, good vibes, people, that's all we're asking, that's our taxation to invest in the soul of the nation. We're here to provide the vibrations to defeat vexations, gooood morning, world.

CEE. We are the sound warriors, the big-tune foragers, the reggae blasters, turntable masters, rhythm riders, vibe providers, groove creators, beat makers, joy investors, dance-hall protectors, welcome welcome all my juicy Lucys, sexy Sashas, yard man and swinging Rastas, here we go!

Lights up in the shop, music fades to the sound of SHELLY*'s headphones.*

The space should be set up like an old-school Caribbean takeaway shop.

SHELLY*, with dustpan and brush in hand, is on her knees cleaning the shop. She is in her own world, enjoying the music.*

CAROL. Shelly. Shelly! SHELLY!

SHELLY *removes her headphones and looks up from her cleaning.*

SHELLY. Why you always shouting?

CAROL. Why yuh never listening? Why yuh sister nuh reach yet?

SHELLY. Do I look like her babysitter? I don't know where she is.

SHELLY *puts her headphones back on.*

CAROL *approaches her and takes her headphones off.* SHELLY *is vex, but it's still her mum, init.*

CAROL. Shelly… call your sister.

SHELLY. You have a phone too!

CAROL *glares at* SHELLY *for a moment until* SHELLY *takes out her phone and dials her sister.*

CHEF *enters and heads towards the kitchen.*

CHEF. Morning, Mrs Hylton.

CAROL. Mmhmm.

SHELLY (*on phone, away from her mother*). She wants to know where you are. Yeah and I do cover for you, but it's getting long, why can't you just get here on time? You said you'd come in and do the clean before open today. Okay fine, but this is the last time.

She hangs up the phone.

She said she'll be a bit late. Victor couldn't take Mya to school, got called into work early so she has to, she's a couple minutes away.

CAROL. Poor boy, that job always working him too hard.

SHELLY. Never mind him, poor Browning, feels like she's a single parent most of the time.

CAROL sits down at one of the tables with a cup of tea. She gets her phone out and starts watching YouTube videos while SHELLY continues preparing the shop for business.

CHEF enters from the kitchen to address CAROL.

CHEF. Mrs Hylton.

CAROL. Yes.

CHEF. I was just wondering if you got my message about next week?

CAROL. Yes.

CHEF. So I was just wondering if you had a chance to read it yet?

CAROL. Yes.

CHEF. So do you think / you could –

CAROL. / No.

CHEF. Okay, no problem, Mrs Hylton.

CHEF exits back to the kitchen.

SHELLY. What was that?

CAROL. What was what?

SHELLY. Why you always have to treat the man like that, Mum? Chef's always doing the most for this place and you talk to him like he doesn't mean nothing to you.

CAROL. I don't remember asking you for your opinion.

SHELLY. All I'm saying is, you could give the guy a break sometimes; or respect, I'm sure he'd appreciate either.

CAROL *continues drinking her tea and watching her videos.*

CAROL. You mean how you show me respect?

SHELLY. Yeah, I do actually. I don't need to be working here you know, I could still be working in London, where I wouldn't need to be on my hands and knees scrubbing the floor like Cinderella. What are you watching?

SHELLY *goes to peek at her phone.* CAROL *covers it.*

CAROL. Do I mek you sleep in the basement?

SHELLY. What?

CAROL. Exactly, you children lie after me like horse a gallop a pasture.

SHELLY. What does that even m– never mind. Mum, I had a chat with the investors again yesterday, they're really keen to talk to us more about / the shop and…

CAROL. I told you already, we don't need no investment. I'm not interested in some suit-wearing man child telling me how to run my business.

SHELLY. Well it's our business now, Mum, remember. And Kelly and Sons is one of the most trusted investment firms in the North West, we should at least hear them out. They sent me the plans of how they think the shop could integrate with the new apartments…

CHEF *re-enters, defiant and bold, slamming the door open interrupting* SHELLY's *flow.*

CHEF. Mrs Hylton. I don't think it's fair that you would say no to me. I just want to borrow the car for one day.

CAROL. That's perfectly reasonable.

CHEF. Then why would you say no?

CAROL. You see the way the two of us are speaking here? Is that so difficult for you?

CHEF. No.

CAROL. Then why do you think it is appropriate to text me and ask me to borrow the car, when I see you in person nearly every day. Don't hide behind your phone like these pickney do, talk to my face… So, do you have something to ask me?

CHEF. Please may I borrow the car next Saturday, Mrs Hylton.

CAROL. Of course you can.

CHEF. Thank you, Carol!

He rushes over to her as if he is about to give her a big kiss. He stops short. Shakes her hand. He walks towards the kitchen. As he does, BROWNING *enters.*

Morning, precious.

CHEF *exits.*

BROWNING. Why's he so happy?

CAROL. Never mind him, getcha apron on, yah late.

BROWNING. Yes, commander.

She hangs up her coat and goes to make herself a cup of tea.

CAROL. Did Mya reach school on time?

BROWNING. Yeah, she did thanks.

CAROL. Just make sure my favourite son-in-law isn't working over the weekend, it's your turn to cook Sunday dinner, remember, and I'm not missing out on Victor's stew chicken.

BROWNING. What's wrong with my stew chicken? Plus, I'm not late, you're early. This nine a.m.-start thing doesn't make any sense. We don't open till eleven.

CAROL. And look at how busy we are when we open, we need to be prepared to serve the people.

SHELLY. Doesn't matter how prepared we are, we're understaffed, this is what I was / trying to say to you, Mum.

CAROL. Well it makes sense to me and it's my shop.

SHELLY. Our shop.

CAROL. Is me one your big head come out of, everything that is yours is mine, so it's my shop.

The sisters mock her behind her back.

SHELLY. You alright, B?

BROWNING. Yeah fine. Mya was vex, obviously, little Daddy's girl. You should see her when he comes home from work, biggest smile ever, but with me, everything's a battle. You'd think I'd burnt down her doll's house the way she looked at me when I said I was taking her to school.

CAROL. You were the same, one likkle Daddy's girl.

BROWNING. No I wasn't.

SHELLY. Are you joking? You know when we were little, Dad was the only one that was allowed to cut up your food, you'd cry if Mum tried to help.

BROWNING. Yeah but that's 'cause she used to hack up the food like she was getting revenge for something.

CAROL. And he was the only one that could calm you down when you were having one of your little meltdowns.

BROWNING. Because he wouldn't call them little meltdowns, he understood the complexity of a young child's emotions, unlike yous two.

SHELLY. It's okay you know, nothing wrong with being a Daddy's girl, just own it. You're a sensitive soul – (*In hushed tones making sure* CAROL *can't hear.*) and that's why you're gonna make a great nursery teacher one day. Speaking of, have you finished the / tests yet?

BROWNING. / Oh allow it, Shelly, not now.

SHELLY. Yes now, if you don't complete the child protection assessments in time, you'll have to start the whole / thing again.

BROWNING. It's fine, I'll do them. By the time I get home from this place and sort Mya out I'm too tired to sit in front of a computer and do some tests like a school kid.

SHELLY. You can't be working here forever.

BROWNING. You're not my careers adviser, you're my baby sister, whether you used to have some fancy job in London or not, so leave it… You look like one, though.

SHELLY. Like what?

BROWNING. A careers adviser, you remember them people that used to come into school. Always in their twenties with the hairstyle of someone in their sixties and clothes that don't fit right.

SHELLY (*laughing with her*). You're out of order.

She attacks BROWNING *with the brush, jokingly, she begins to chase her around the shop.*

CAROL. You two finish play fool yet? Shelly, come show me how this foolish machine works again.

CAROL holds up the contactless card machine. One of them slim smartphone-looking ones. It beeps and says 'disconnected'. SHELLY heads toward her to help.

SHELLY. It's basically the same as the last one, Mum, it just means that we can operate it ourselves and don't get charged out the arse when it breaks.

CAROL. Language.

SHELLY. Sorry, it means we don't have to pay a hefty sum of our hard-earned British pounds when it becomes faulty. Better.

CAROL (*kissed teeth*). The cheek of this one here, why does it keep saying disconnected at me? Let me just use the old one, nuh?

SHELLY *fiddles with the machine, fixing it.*

SHELLY. The old one is outdated, Mum, the buttons didn't even press down properly, we were selling ten pounds worth of food for one pound by accident, you'll get used to this one.

It beeps: 'Connected'. She hands it back to CAROL.

RICHARD *enters.*

RICHARD. Good morning, B.

BROWNING. Morning, Richard.

BROWNING *and* RICHARD *share a little handshake.*

RICHARD. Good morning, Mrs Hylton.

CAROL. The shop nuh open yet.

SHELLY. It's Richard, Mum.

CAROL *looks up at him.*

CAROL. Oh.

CHEF *enters.*

CHEF (*in a scouse accent*). Yes Richard, lad!

An uncomfortable silence for a moment.

RICHARD. Chef, what you got for me today, lad?

CHEF. Ya, ackee and saltfish is on the way, my friend.

RICHARD. Ah you make my days so much easier. You good yeah?

CHEF. Me good man, s'far.

CHEF *exits to kitchen.*

SHELLY. Busy day today?

RICHARD. Yeah, couple meetings in the morning with some families round Granby then just back in the office. If I can get in them, you seen those crowds building on Parli?

SHELLY. What crowds?

RICHARD. The protests over those developers that want to build on the field next door. I'm gonna head down there after work if you wanna join?

SHELLY. Sounds romantic, but no. We've spoken about this, you know I don't agree with the protests, bunch of people that don't understand business.

RICHARD. Bunch of people that care about this community… what time you finishing here today?

SHELLY. Late. I'm filming some more content for the shop's TikTok.

RICHARD. Yeah well don't stay too late, you've worked wonders with the shop so far.

SHELLY. Try telling her that. Plus look at me, I'm fine!

RICHARD. Indeed, you look healthy as ever, my love.

He moves toward her in a seductive way. She pulls away after a moment.

SHELLY. Wait, you saying I look fat.

CHEF *enters and senses* RICHARD's *in trouble.*

CHEF. Bon appetite.

RICHARD. Thank you, I'll catch up with you later, yeah.

SHELLY. Yeah sounds good.

Beat.

Do you really have to go to the protests?

RICHARD. Shelly!

SHELLY. Fine, but don't get sucked into doing anything stupid.

RICHARD (*cheekily*). Who me? Never!

He exits.

CAROL. Where does Raymond work again?

SHELLY. Richard, Mum, and he works for a housing agency, you know that.

CAROL. Estate agent?

SHELLY. No he works with people that need help in social housing, Mum, we've spoken about this before.

BROWNING. You must remember Richard, Mum, Charlie's lad.

CAROL. Yes of course, sorry. Team meeting in one minute.

She exits to the kitchen, ushering CHEF *that way too.*

BROWNING. Awkward.

SHELLY. Shut up.

I don't get why she's got such an issue with him. Since when did anyone around here care about who was dating who? Liverpool's like the unofficial interracial relationship capital of the world. Now I come back and all of a sudden it's a problem with Richard. It's all these weird YouTube videos she's been watching; I saw her watching a Dr Umar video the other day you know.

BROWNING. Well maybe if you spent less time with Richard and more time with her outside the shop, she wouldn't spend all day on YouTube.

SHELLY. We're together every day. Now hurry up, finish cleaning before the meeting.

BROWNING. Stop deflecting. Look, I don't care who you date, I don't have to date him.

SHELLY. Yeah and neither does Mum.

BROWNING. She's just doing the whole protective mum thing.

Beat.

What's he saying though, you know, down there?

SHELLY. Excuse you?

BROWNING. You know, down there, I've never been with a white man before, so I don't know, but you know what they say init.

She wiggles her little finger.

SHELLY. I swear.

She chases BROWNING *like she is going to attack her playfully.* BROWNING *goes over to the radio and turns it on. 'Whine and Kotch' by Charly Black and J Capri plays (the dirtiest moment of the song).* BROWNING *trys to get* SHELLY *to dance and loosen herself up, she starts playfully pushing her backside into her.* CAROL *enters from the kitchen,* CHEF *following behind her.*

CAROL. Browning, turn that duttiness off.

BROWNING. Come dance with us.

CAROL. Browning, please stop fooling around, for once.

BROWNING *begrudgingly turns the radio off.*

Alright come around.   SHELLY. Okay let's get started.

They look at each other awkwardly for a moment.

They all come and sit around CAROL's *table.*

Who's first?

CHEF. Everything the same in the kitchen. My food is flying out the door, of course! Oxtail – ah sell out, curry goat – ah sell out, ackee and saltfish – ah sell out, patties – ah sell out. Everything ah sell, Mrs Hylton, as expected.

SHELLY. The patties are still too cheap, Mum.

CAROL. Is it your turn to speak yet? Chef, continue please.

CHEF. That's it actually.

CAROL. Okay, thank you. Shelly?

SHELLY. We have two weddings and a birthday party next week, oh and we just booked a funeral on Saturday too. Janette said she's free to come and help me out with those so we're okay for staff.

CAROL. Any more booked in for the rest of the month.

SHELLY. A couple yeah. I updated the website and put a few ads on Facebook banners and things like that. They target people in the area and people that click on Caribbean-related things so it should hopefully be quite useful. We can charge higher prices for the catering, which is good.

CAROL. Okay, anything else?

SHELLY. Ummm what else. I've upped our Supermalt orders, I think the hipsters have discovered it, so it's selling quite well.

BROWNING. Yeah Tescos even sell it in their 'ethnic' aisle now.

CAROL. You didn't ask me about ordering more Supermalt.

SHELLY. I didn't know I had to.

Awkward silence.

I've started taking a look at portion sizes as well. If you won't up the prices in here then we're gonna have to stop loading up the plates like we have been, we're barely breaking even. I should be able to get some suggestions to you by the end of the week about what's sustainable and what gradual price increases might feel comfortable for you.

CAROL. No it's fine I can do that.

SHELLY. No it's okay, Mum, I'm happy to. I know that stuff pretty well. That type of analysis is one of the things I really enjoyed at my last job so I should be able / to get –

CAROL. / I will do it. This isn't your flash city job, it's a takeaway, we sell food.

SHELLY. Okay, passive. But to be honest, Mum, the catering is keeping this place open and us fed, the shop isn't bringing enough in. I think we should talk / about the proposal.

CAROL. / No.

SHELLY. Mum, come on, we have to keep up with the times. We're a business, not a soup kitchen, we might be busy but we're basically giving the food away for free. But if we partner with Kelly and Sons we could.

CAROL. I said no.

SHELLY. Look at all them places in the Baltic market, them little pop-up places, they're always busy, always buzzing, its an occasion, people are willing to pay proper money! We need to provide an experience. And we can only do that with Kelly and Sons, the amount they're offering is huge, like retirement huge, and they / think if we –

CAROL. I don't care, Shelly, We are not selling this shop to be swallowed up by them flats. Let's move on, please.

SHELLY. A lick of paint, some new furniture, just 'cause everything around here looks like it's crumbling, doesn't mean our shop has to as well. With their investment, a new shop and all the customers that would be living in the flats / we would –

BROWNING. If anyone can afford to live in them, girl.

SHELLY. Look, I took the liberty of having one of my friends who knows design draw up these examples of what the shop could look like.

SHELLY *pulls out a portfolio of images and renders of a revamped shop.*

It's really simple, some small changes can make a huge difference. I even made these.

She pulls her top up and reveals a shirt with the shop's logo on it.

I've got one for all of you.

She pulls a bunch of T-shirts out of a bag. BROWNING *takes one enthusiastically.* CAROL *snatches it from her.*

CAROL. What are you doing? I am not turning your dad's shop into one of them places, yah understand? That's the end of it.

SHELLY. It's our shop now, Mum, he left it to me and you, and if we don't do something, *Dad's* shop is going to die.

There is an awkward silence for a moment until it's too much and BROWNING *tries to break it.*

BROWNING. I can finally use the till properly now! Chef gave me lessons, he's a much better teacher than you, Shelly, doesn't use all your dumb metaphors.

SHELLY. What dumb metaphors?

BROWNING. The one about the till being like a Hobnob?

SHELLY. If you were paying attention, it would have made sense.

CAROL. Anything else, Browning?

BROWNING. Nah that's it.

CAROL. Okay, back to work – (*Under her breath.*) Dear Lord help me.

BROWNING heads straight to the till, CHEF to the kitchen. CAROL and SHELLY stay sat at the table. The noise of a group of people moving past the shop is heard. SHELLY looks out the window at them.

SHELLY. These people, man.

CAROL. What people?

SHELLY. All these idiots running through the streets hooded up. Look at those, headed straight for the police looking for a fight, for what?

CAROL. For their livelihoods, Shelly. We're being pushed out of this place. All these suits coming round and buying the whole place up. And you want to just hand this place over to them.

SHELLY. It's just business, Mum. Should have sold that land next door off sooner if you ask me, it's an eyesore. Just 'cause some land gets sold, doesn't mean people should be breaking shop windows and rioting? Half of those kids out there aren't even from the area, opportunists.

CAROL. Uprising! Not rioting. There is a difference between rioting and rising up. You wouldn't understand.

SHELLY. No I do understand, Mum, I understand that our 'people' have been sucked into some ignorant fight by themselves, rioting and looting shops for free shit, like always.

CAROL. Like I say, *you* wouldn't understand.

Beat.

SHELLY. What's that supposed to mean?

CAROL. Ever since I sent you to that school in Crosby… they been in your head.

SHELLY. Who's they?

CAROL. You know what I mean.

BROWNING. In her knickers now too.

SHELLY. Shut up, B. are you serious mum?

CAROL. I'm not talking about Raymond.

SHELLY. Richard.

CAROL. I'm not talking about *him*; I'm saying you just don't understand any more, you don't understand your people.

SHELLY. My 'people'? What because I don't agree with senseless violence I don't understand my 'people'. (*She physically does the inverted commas.*)

CAROL. And because you talk about your people in inverted commas every time.

SHELLY. Because it's ridiculous, Mum. When did you turn into some wannabe Black Panther? This is L8, not LA, it's

never been black and white like that – (*To* BROWNING.)
She watches the *Black Messiah* once and thinks she's
Malcolm X.

She looks to BROWNING *to try and get involved in the joke.*

CAROL. I'm not laughing with you. Don't lecture me about
Liverpool. You ran away as soon as you could. Listen, I just
know Russell isn't a good match for you.

SHELLY. Richard! And how do you know who is a good match
for... I thought this wasn't about him?

CAROL. It's not, it's about you. I just think in a time like this,
with all the things I'm seeing on the news and YouTube / you
shoul–

SHELLY. / I swear, there should be an age cap for who's
allowed to watch YouTube.

CAROL. No, I'm being serious, Shelly, I was watching... wah
dem call it... Novara Media / and they...

SHELLY. / Oh come on, Mum.

CAROL. Listen, I'm allowed to have my opinions, and
I think, if I'm really being honest with myself... a black
woman should be with a black man. A white man will
never understand a black woman truly, even in Liverpool,
especially a black woman who doesn't understand herself.

SHELLY. But if I was with one of those boys out there
smashing the place up, as long as he was one of the black
ones, that would be okay? He understands me a lot more
than you do or clearly ever will, how can you tell me what he
understands when you can't even remember his name!

CAROL. Me nah care what him name is. You think because he
eats some ackee he's part of this community? He is not part
of this / community –

SHELLY. / His whole family is from Toxteth, he was born and
raised here, he's more a part of this community than you /
what are you talking about?

CAROL. / One day you will understand how your 'people' have been pushed to this point.

SHELLY. Now who's using fucking inverted commas. I'm going for a walk.

SHELLY exits, absolutely fucking furious. A silence in the shop after her exit.

CAROL. I used the commas on purpose then.

Silence.

BROWNING. You two ever agree on anything?

CHEF. Them both like my oxtail.

CHEF laughs to himself, hoping the others will join in with the joke. They don't. He busies himself with something.

BROWNING. But you never listen to her, Mum, sometimes she has a point… occasionally, sometimes. She just doesn't always say things in the right way. You two used to be like best mates before she moved to London, now it's like watching an episode of *Game of Thrones* with you two.

CAROL. New broom sweep clean but ole broom know di corners…

BROWNING. No, Mum, it's not time for one of your old proverbs. I've looked at some of her ideas for the shop. If utilities are going up I think –

CAROL. We're doing just fine, don't you be worrying about that.

BROWNING. Liverpool's changing, Mum. Maybe we should put the prices up a bit, people want to support us. Down at Baltic I once saw a patty for four pound!

CHEF spits his drink out dramatically.

CHEF. FOUR POUND! Did you get insurance on it too?

CAROL. I'm not robbing from the people dem. We're doing just fine, Browning, don't worry.

BROWNING. Mmhmm.

CAROL. Excuse me?

BROWNING. I said fine.

CAROL. Facety gal.

Beat.

Chef, why you just standing round? You think I pay you to read newspaper? Cook suttin nah, man.

CHEF (*trying to joke, playfully*). Relax nah man, I'm an artiste, I cook when the cooking takes me.

CAROL. Me said cook!

Beat.

CHEF. Yes, Mrs Hylton.

CHEF *exits to the kitchen.*

BROWNING. Mum!

BROWNING *too exits to the kitchen.* CAROL *pulls out some letters and begins to read them, she looks stressed. It is hot, and reading the letters is making her hotter. The contactless machine beeps again and says 'disconnected'. She has had enough, and she heads towards the kitchen ripping out and disconnecting the contactless machine aggressively as she passes to go through to the kitchen.*

SHELLY *enters the shop again; she stormed out without taking her coat.*

As she goes to get her coat, she looks at all the letters on the table, flicking through them. She takes her coat, takes out her phone and dials.

SHELLY. Hey, this is Shelly calling, can I be put through to the Kelly and Sons office, please.

SHELLY *exits. We enter the radio station.*

CEE. Welcome back, people, just a quick news update for you.

TC. Yes we are hearing that the protests are getting a bit nasty out there. So far there have been twenty arrests and parts of Upper Parliament Street are currently blocked off near the Rialto.

CEE. As soon as we hear more, you'll hear more.

TC. For now, keep enjoying the tunes and keep working hard wherever you are.

'Israelites' by Desmond Dekker & the Aces plays.

Scene Two

End of Day One.

BROWNING *is in the shop on her phone. She is packing everything down as she speaks.*

BROWNING. Hiya, how's work? What time you gonna be home? Victor, seriously? Can't someone else just do it? Well will you be there in the morning to take Mya to school? Victor, I work as well you know. Of course I love being with her, what does that even mean? You're her dad… I know we need money, obviously, that's not the point. Do you even like spending time with us? You know what, it's not that deep, whatever, I'll speak to you later, tara. Love you… I said love you…

She hangs up. She pulls her laptop out and starts doing some work on it for her childcare course. CHEF *enters.*

CHEF. You studying hard?

BROWNING. Something like that. Some of the questions they ask are so stupid. I have my own child, I know how to keep them alive. I don't even know if I want to do it yano. Not sure I can leave Mum and Shelly running this shop together.

CHEF. You can't worry about them, I'll be here. You'll be alright, precious.

BROWNING *laughs to herself.*

What you laughing at?

BROWNING. Precious. It's funny how you always call me precious, like you're in some nineteen fifties rom-com.

CHEF. Is that an insult? You know I don't watch films too much.

BROWNING. No it's cute. Don't know why you're always calling me precious though, nothing precious about me. Can't even finish a test that's made for sixteen-year-olds straight out of school.

CHEF. You're too hard on yuhself… You are precious.

BROWNING. Why?

CHEF. The way you are with your mum and your sister.

BROWNING. What do you mean?

CHEF. You just…. hold them together, Mrs Hylton and Shelly would have killed each other by now if it wasn't for you.

BROWNING. Exactly! And here I am tryna find a way to get a job somewhere else, I'm selfish. This shop is breaking this family. Sometimes I just wanna burn it down and start all over again.

CHEF. Raaahhhhtiidd. You British pickney are so dramatic – (*Kisses his teeth.*) Listen, you have to live your own life. If yuh spend the whole time trying to make other people happy, you'll make yourself miserable. But the gift you have. The skill to make other people smile and feel better, that's precious, to me anyway.

BROWNING. Err. Are you hitting on me, Chef?

CHEF. Nooooo, no. You is like me daughter, just wanna big you up.

BROWNING. Thanks, Chef. I guess I am a bit precious init. You ain't too bad yourself you know, Chef.

CHEF. Thank you! Here, I got something I want you to try.

He's goes to the kitchen and pulls out a dish to present
BROWNING *with.*

Try this.

BROWNING. What is it?

CHEF. It's a dish I been working on. I entered this competition, made it to the final in Leeds next week, that's why I wanted to borrow the car. If I won, I would have had the dish stocked in supermarkets for two months.

BROWNING. What, that's incredible, why didn't you tell us about it?

CHEF. Ah, me cyant go. That funeral we booked to cater is on the same day, so I'll have to do that instead, and we'll need the car for that so… stop wid the questions, try the food nah man.

BROWNING *takes a mouthful of the dish.*

BROWNING. Oh my god, Chef, that is boss! What is that?

CHEF. Secret recipe, me cyant give away my secrets for you to go sell it to my competition.

BROWNING. Honestly, Chef, that is incredible. You have to go to the final; you can't not go because of one catering gig.

CHEF. Who else gan cook? You? *This* is my job, *that* is a dream, I'll have plenty of time to dream later.

BROWNING. No, Chef, seriously / you need to.

CHEF. / It's okay. Thank you… precious.

BROWNING. Why do you stay here, Chef, why don't you go and do your own thing, you're incredible. You know Mum will never let you serve food like this here, what does she always say.

CHEF *and* BROWNING. Stick to the basics, food nah need a facelift.

CHEF. No I couldn't. When I first reach here, your mother and father were the only people to even think about giving me a job. I owe them a lot.

SHELLY. What did you just say to me about making other people happy?

CHEF. I am happy. I cook me likkle food, I pay my bills, I'm bless.

SHELLY *enters from the kitchen.*

SHELLY. Eurgh, get me out of this place.

SHELLY *walks over to* BROWNING *and takes a mouthful of the dish in front of her.*

Mmmmm that's banging, what you two yapping about?

BROWNING *goes to respond,* CAROL *enters before she can.*

CAROL. Alright, that's closing time.

CAROL *goes to exit.*

SHELLY. Oh, Mum, can you just sign the bottom of this for me please?

CAROL. What is it?

SHELLY. It's just the agreement for next week's catering at the Palm House.

CAROL *signs.*

CAROL. Alright, me gaan, Unu lock up properly ya hear.

CHEF. Yes, Mrs Hylton.

CAROL *exits.*

SHELLY *and* BROWNING (*mockingly*). Yes, Mrs Hylton –

They laugh.

CHEF. You laugh away, the boss isn't mother to all of us you know, I have to work to keep my job.

SHELLY. That's the reason she's the way she is you know, you have to challenge her sometimes.

BROWNING. Maybe you challenge her a bit too much! Maybe try being her daughter again for a bit.

SHELLY. Please, you two definitely don't challenge her enough.

BROWNING. It's not everyday challenge, some days just talk you know. You seeing Richard tonight?

SHELLY. Yes. Going to that new Italian place in town then chilling.

BROWNING. I'm glad you two reconnected, I always knew you'd end up together in the end. Better than that dickhead boyfriend you had in London – (*Mocking posh accent.*) Hi, I'm Quiton, investment banker at Wankers limited.

SHELLY. We all have… blips. / I'm glad we reconnected too.

BROWNING. / The fuck is a blip?

SHELLY. He's still tryna make sure we have regular date nights, and it gives me a good chance to check out the competition.

BROWNING. Always working.

CHEF. You shoulda told me it was date night, I coulda set you up a nice little romantic table in the back with some candles and proper food.

SHELLY. Careful I might take you up on the offer one day.

CHEF. Any time, darling, I like that boy of yours. Come we go, we all walking together?

SHELLY. Nah, Richard's meeting me here, you go though, B.

BROWNING. Cool.

BROWNING *collects her jacket and bag and heads to the door.*

In a bit, lil sis.

SHELLY. See you later, B, Chef you meeting me in the morning yeah?

CHEF. Same time same place.

SHELLY. Bye.

> SHELLY *waits for them to leave, then heads over to the radio and switches it on.*

CEE. Welcome to lovers' hour, hold your loved ones tight, don't let them out of sight, keep warm for the night, we're here to get you in the mood, let's start off with this one, Colours, spin that.

> *'Brown Skin' by Richie Spice starts playing.* SHELLY *creeps over to the door and opens it for* RICHARD. *He enters and gives her a warm embrace.*

RICHARD. I've missed you today.

SHELLY. What? The whole big healthy me?

RICHARD. Oh come on, Shelly.

SHELLY. I'm playing, I've missed you too.

RICHARD. How was work?

SHELLY (*sheepishly*). Yeah it was fine thanks, how about you?

RICHARD. A bit long actually. I went to meet a client that just refuses to help himself. We've been bending over backwards to get him housing but the councils just longing it out.

I don't know what else we can do. They keep trying to move him out of the city, but his daughter's here.

SHELLY. Sorry.

RICHARD. It's alright, we'll figure it out.

SHELLY. Did you go to those protests in the end? It sounds like it's getting a bit hectic out there.

RICAHRD (*sheepishly*). Ahh, yeah, just for a moment but I didn't stay long.

SHELLY. Richard… This isn't college or uni and your little Antifa society any more you know, it's not just a slap on the wrist if you do something stupid, there's a lot of police out there.

RICHARD. I just went by there for a moment, I'm here, aren't I?

SHELLY. I'm serious, Richard, I know how you feel about the developments, we agreed to disagree, but that doesn't mean I'm happy with you getting in trouble over it.

RICHARD. If I remember correctly, in college you were out at every protest with me. In fact, if I remember correctly, you were the one that first stood outside of Wayne's house when they came and tried to deport him, encouraging everyone to make a wall around the house.

SHELLY. Yeah and I was also the one that wrote the letter of support that ended up *actually* helping him with his right to remain.

RICHARD. Okay, I won't go back. I promise.

SHELLY. Good. Good…

RICHARD. Okay. Come here.

He pulls her closer.

I've been thinking about tonight all day.

He goes to kiss her but she turns her head.

What's wrong?

SHELLY. Nothing I'm fine.

RICHARD. What is this 'I'm fine' thing you always do? I can see you're not fine, talk to me.

SHELLY. No honestly, it's fine.

He looks at her.

It's just… with Mum. I can't get anything through to her, it's like it's impossible for her to listen.

RICHARD. Why?

SHELLY. I don't know, it's just the way she is.

RICHARD. Just the way she is, or…

SHELLY. What?

RICHARD. Well, like just now, I have to ask like five questions before I get a real answer. Everything's always just fine. How's your day? Fine. How's work? Fine.

How's the middle east, fine. I love you babe, sometimes its just a battle to actually get you to talk.

SHELLY. I'm talking to you now.

RICHARD. Maybe you should talk to your mum more instead of having to talk to me about her. I'm not saying don't talk to me, I'm always here when you need to vent but it's no use just storing shit up to explode to me, then building it back up when you're with her. You two never really listen to each other, it's always an argument or some strange point-scoring game. Maybe you also don't listen to her.

SHELLY. Whose side are you on? if I listened to her we wouldn't be together.

RICHARD. Okay, I'm not saying do everything she says or agree with every word that leaves her mouth, trust me I'm really not saying that. I'm just saying, try to have conversations, not fights.

SHELLY. It doesn't work that way, you wouldn't understand.

RICHARD. Try me.

SHELLY. It's just… different for us. We don't talk about emotions and stuff, we don't sit down and talk about how we're feeling, bla… our family don't really do that. And with her everything's just ten times harder, she just shuts me down, it's always been like that.

RICHARD. Hmm, sounds familiar.

SHELLY. Oh fuck off.

RICHARD. Look I'm just saying maybe you two aren't so different.

Silence, moment for SHELLY *to think.*

I bought you something.

He pulls two tickets out of his bag and gives them to her.

SHELLY. Oh… wow… two tickets to see… The Bob Marley tribute band at the Playhouse… thanks.

RICHARD. Bad gift?

SHELLY. No it's… yeah, bad gift… sorry. A Bob Marley tribute band?

RICHARD. I just thought… 'cause you are… you like…

SHELLY. You've got a lot to learn, white boy.

She laughs and gives him a hug.

I'm serious about the protests, Richard. Don't go back. I've been… I've been talking to Kelly and Sons. Nothing's finalised yet but we might be working with them in some way and I don't want you caught up in all that.

RICHARD. What do you mean working with them?

SHELLY. This shop is… we're struggling, and they're offering us a way out, I can't see any other way. Dad left the shop to me and Mum because he knew I would make the decisions we need to.

RICHARD. Shelly, you know how important those footy pitches are to this community, we can't let them build over them. You can't work with them, Shelly. You can't support that. I know we said we agree to disagree about the protests, but you can't… you can't be a part of that, Shelly. You grew up here.

SHELLY. What's the alternative?

RICHARD. What's the alterna– Surely your mum hasn't agreed to working with them?

SHELLY. She's… thinking about it.

RICHARD. Shelly…

SHELLY. Let's not talk about it. Come on, we're gonna be late for our reservation, let's just go have a good night.

RICHARD. Is it a joke, are you joking…?

SHELLY. Let's just go have a nice time.

> *She reaches for* RICHARD. *He moves away and exits the shop. As he opens the door, we hear the noise of escalating tension from outside, it's bubbling but hasn't spilled into the shop yet.* SHELLY *is left alone.*

Scene Three

Day Two.

CAROL *is in the shop watching YouTube again.* SHELLY *enters. They do not speak.* SHELLY *takes off her jacket and puts down her bag. She goes to the back to collect her apron. As she comes back she turns the radio on. 'Thank U Mamma' by Sizzla is playing. She begins to wipe down the counters. She moves onto the table* CAROL *is sitting at.* SHELLY *stares at* CAROL *until she picks up her cup of tea to wipe the table. She carries on doing different chores until she gets fed up with the music and changes the station. The first few lines of 'Mama' by Alaine plays, she changes again. 'Mama' by Christopher Martin then plays, then 'Mama' by Vybz Kartel. She turns off the radio.*

SHELLY. Eurgh.

> BROWNING *enters and recognises the tension.*

BROWNING. Sorry I can't work today, I need to finish this childcare assessment, just coming to pick up Mya's tablet, I think she left it here.

CAROL. I don't know why you're still doing those tests, you won't have time to have another job and still work here.

BROWNING. Just good to have another qualification, Mum, safety net.

CAROL. Mmhmm.

There is a strange atmosphere BROWNING *can sense.*

BROWNING (*cautiously*). Everyone okay?

Silence.

OOOkkay. Anybody want to talk about this?

Nothing.

Okay, I'll rephrase that. Both of you come and sit here, we're talking about this.

CAROL *and* SHELLY *stand still for a moment then reluctantly come and sit at the table.*

Okay, that's a start. So what's the problem?

SHELLY. I don't have a problem, ask her.

CAROL. 'Her' is your mother and you will address me as such.

BROWNING. Okay... we're talking, that's good. So what is Mum's problem, Shelly?

SHELLY. *Her* problem is that she is stuck in the past. She thinks she's still in Jamaica, you moved here when you were nine, Mum, you're more British than Jamaican now. Don't think I don't hear you with your real accent when you go to town. 'Hiya, Sheila, love, did ya watch the footy today, hun?'

CAROL. You see, that is *her* problem. All her friends at uni and in London have corrupted her, talking to me any kind of way, thinking she can make decisions about my shop without me. It's second-generation kids, I was watching a video / about it.

SHELLY. / This is stupid I'm off.

BROWNING. Uh uh uh. I didn't dismiss you. D'ya know what, it's getting really boring hearing you two go back and forth with each other so we're sorting it. This shop is tearing you two apart and it ends now.

SHELLY. I don't have time to listen to her racist shit.

CAROL. You see what I mean, listen to her. I didn't raise a child to swear at her mother.

SHELLY. Well you did, 'cause she's sitting right here. Be proud that you raised a child to challenge all the crap you were brought up believing. I'm so sorry for trying to break the generational trauma you did your best to hand down to me.

CAROL. What did she call me? A generational who? This is pointless, Browning, I can't make her love her mother.

SHELLY. Oh my days, how old are you? Don't try and be all victimy now.

CAROL. My god, if your father could see you now.

SHELLY. Don't you dare, Mum… Dad left the shop to both of us for a reason. If he thought you could do this yourself, he wouldn't have left it to me too. Look, thanks for your efforts, B, but we're just gonna have to agree to disagree and / that's fine.

BROWNING. No, we're not. Look, Shelly. All Mum wants is the best for you. She might not be able to show that all the time, but it's true. She doesn't want you getting hurt.

She's been around for aaages.

CAROL. Hexcuse you?

BROWNING. She's seen the bad things that people do and she doesn't want it to happen to you. You know how hard she's had to work to be where we are, she doesn't want you to get hurt by people that might not care about you. And, Mum, sometimes you need to listen to Shelly more. You raised a smart girl and she has a point… sometimes. We live in a different time than you did, you have to adjust to that a little. And Shelly's right, Mum, all this race stuff is strange, it's never been like that around here, you never used to be like this. Not all white people are bad… just some of them, okay?

CAROL. I know, it's true, maybe I should listen to you more. You girls have grown up in a different world to me. I love you, Shelly, and I only want what's best for you. And I know that isn't that likkle eejit boy Robert.

SHELLY. Ahh here we fucking go.

They start arguing and shouting over each other.

BROWNING (*shouting over them*). IF YOU TWO DON'T STOP, I QUIT.

Beat. SHELLY *and* CAROL *look at her, then kiss their teeth in unison and go back to arguing.*

CHEF *enters.*

CHEF. Ladies, ladies, please. This can't continue.

CAROL. Is who asked you? And what time you call this? Your shift started five minutes ago, gwan cook suttin.

CHEF exits, *CAROL heads to the kitchen.*

BROWNING. Shelly, man, that wasn't right, you can't be talking to Mum like that.

SHELLY. Well how should I talk to her, B? She doesn't listen to anything I say, she's like a stubborn child.

BROWNING. What and you're not? You listen to what she says do you? You don't even let each other finish before you start shouting over each other, how can either of you be listening to each other when you don't even hear what the other says?

SHELLY. So what do you want me to do, B? Just say 'Yes, Mum', 'Sorry Mum', 'Can I have some more please, Mum?' She doesn't accept who I date. She doesn't accept how I talk. She doesn't accept my friends. She was happy for me to go to uni to study business, telling all her friends about her smart, successful daughter, but won't let me help with our business. That was never her strong suit, it was Dad that ran this shop, not Mum. The shop is dying, B, and she won't even let me help.

BROWNING. We're not dying, Shelly, the shop is still busy, everyone loves this place, everyone loves Hyltons!

SHELLY *goes and gets the letters* CAROL *has been hiding.*

SHELLY. Look: late mortgage payment, gas and lecky chasing us. 'Overdue credit for stock', 'food hygiene licence up for renewal'. We're drowning. She's drowning and she's too fucking stubborn to even talk about it. All the accounts are in her name so I can't even get in to sort it out.

BROWNING. Yeah but that's just her thing, Shelly. She don't wanna talk about it. You know Mum will sort it, she always does, we'll be fine, Mum will just fix everything in her own way.

SHELLY. No, B, Dad fixed things, Dad sorted things. We can't just hope for the best any more. When we were kids we didn't know any different but now I can see it how am I supposed to just ignore it?

BROWNING. What's wrong with you, Shelly, talking about Mum like she was just some helpless little woman that just did what Dad said?

CAROL *appears from the kitchen and lingers, unseen by the sisters.*

SHELLY. She was, B! You don't remember, or you ignored it, but she was. But I'm not her. I know what I'm doing and I know what this shop needs. She's stuck in the past, and it's never going to be like that again.

BROWNING. Give her some grace, Shelly. She lost her husband

SHELLY. We lost our dad too, you know…

I'm going for a walk before the shop opens.

SHELLY *takes off her apron and exits.* CAROL *enters and sees* BROWNING *at the table looking at all of the letters.*

BROWNING. Mum…

CAROL. I thought you said you're not working today, get your things and go, I'll see you tomorrow, don't be late.

BROWNING. But, Mum.

CAROL. Hurry up, Browning!

BROWNING. Why are we doing this, Mum? This shop is pushing you and Shelly further and further apart, is it worth it? It isn't making us any money. What are all these bills and notices? Maybe we should just sell the shop, start fresh, do what you actually want to do, be a family, not a business. Who are we doing this for?

CAROL *doesn't respond.*

Mum...

CAROL. LEAVE!

BROWNING *collects her things and exits.* CAROL *heads to the kitchen.*

Scene Four

Day Two. Evening.

CEE. Welcome back, beautiful people, we're keeping the vibes going for you this Friday night, getting you ready for your weekend. Let us know what you're doing, keep the texts coming in.

TC. Yes I have a message here from sexybrownskin who says 'touching down at Southbeach club this evening with the girls #turnup'

CEE. badmanjulio says 'looking to bend over a phat pus–'

TC. Whooooa whoa whoa, thank you for that one, badmanjulio. Cee, you have to screen these messages, man.

CEE. Sorry about that, let us know what you're doing.

TC. Yes yes, in other news we're hearing that police are looking for a man that was causing some trouble at the protests today. Apparently he broke into the building of developers Kelly and Sons and set fire to the office!

CEE. Haha at least my man's taking the fight straight to the source, not like these youts out here mashing up the boulevard.

> SHELLY *and* RICHARD *enter the shop.* RICHARD *is bleeding. They stumble around in the dark for a little bit. They find the light and switch it on.* RICHARD *is in pain and grunting.*

SHELLY. Go sit over there, let me look for some towels.

> SHELLY *goes to look for something to tend to his wounds. She finds a towel and presses it on* RICHARD'*s bleeding hand. He screeches.*

> BROWNING *enters the front door.*

> Browning!

BROWNING. Shelly.

SHELLY. What the fuck are you doing here?

BROWNING. I wanted somewhere quiet to do my assessments.

SHELLY. Why have you got all your bags with you?

BROWNING. 'Cause I do. What are yous doing here?

SHELLY. Shhhh, stop being so loud!

BROWNING. What's wrong with your hand, Richard, are you bleeding?

SHELLY. Never, it's fucking ketchup. Yes, he's bleeding, go to the kitchen and get me some towels.

> BROWNING *heads towards the kitchen. As she gets close to the door,* CHEF *enters from the kitchen in a cloud of weed smoke, dressed in boxers and a vest, holding a roll of cling film like a weapon.*

CHEF. What's all this shouting about?

ALL. CHEF!

CHEF. Richard, what the hell happen to you, man?

RICHARD. I... ermmm.

SHELLY. Never mind him, why are you still here?

BROWNING. Are you homeless?

CHEF. No, me nah homeless... I was just... erm, you see
I was –

CAROL *enters in some sort of night clothing or something
indicating she was intimate with* CHEF *and places a hand on
his shoulder.*

CAROL. Chef, what is going on out here...

She notices the full room.

SHELLY *and* BROWNING. MUM!

CAROL. What is happening in my shop, why is Ralph bleeding
on my floor?

RICHARD. Charming.

SHELLY *and* CAROL. Shut up, Richard/Ronny.

BROWNING. Mum, why are you here?

CAROL. It's my shop, I can be here when I want, why are you
here

SHELLY. ...Were you back there with Chef?

CAROL *and* CHEF *look at each other.*

CAROL. We were just figuring out what stock we need to order.

CHEF. Yes, we were... calculating numbers... mathematics.

SHELLY. Partially dressed and in a cloud of smoke?

CAROL. You see what I mean, Browning, see how she talk to
me.

BROWNING. Nope, you're on your own with this one, Mum.

CAROL. Listen just get out my shop, all ah yuh.

SHELLY. No wait, Mum, we can't.

CAROL. What do you mean you can't? Me said come outta me
shop nah, man.

SHELLY. No listen, Mum, Richard's in trouble we can't –

CAROL. I can see he's in trouble and it's none of my business, come outta me shop.

SHELLY. No, Mum, wait, it's the police, they're looking for him.

CAROL. So he's a criminal as well, there's more wrong with you than I thought, child!

SHELLY. Mum, please you can't kick us out. He was out there fighting for all that shit you believe in like a fool.

CAROL. Wah you mean.

SHELLY. He was at those bloody riots –

CAROL/CHEF/BROWNING/RICHARD. Uprisings –

SHELLY. – it went a bit… far.

CAROL. But wait, it's you they're talking about on the news? The one who broke into Kelly and Sons?

RICHARD. Ah… yes.

SHELLY. Please, Mum.

CAROL. Just clean up yourself and get out, I'll give you half an hour.

SHELLY and RICHARD head to the kitchen. CHEF tries to hand CAROL a shirt, she pushes it away. Silence for a moment.

BROWNING. You and Chef, Mum?

CAROL. Don't you dare, Browning.

More silence.

BROWNING. Nah, it's cool, Mum, no judgement here. It's 2025. Women need love at all ages.

CAROL. Browning…

Silence for a bit.

BROWNING. Were you smoking, too?

CAROL. Browning!

BROWNING. Sorry, sorry… is he my new dad?

CAROL *raises her hand like she's ready to backhand* BROWNING.

SHELLY *and* RICHARD *return.*

SHELLY. Thank you, Mum.

CAROL. Don't thank me, just sort yourself out quick.

RICHARD. Thank you, Mrs Hylton.

CAROL. Mmhmm.

SHELLY *either switches on the TV, or turns on the radio.* [*Whatever you prefer, if there's a TV in the space use that, or if you want to imagine it in the audience, or use the radio if it doesn't feel too strange that they're getting their news from the radio in this day and age!*]

PRESENTER. Police are still looking for a key instigator in tonight's disturbances in Liverpool.

Police tell us they are looking for a male, wearing an all-black tracksuit of average height.

RICHARD. Average height?

SHELLY. Shhhhh.

PRESENTER. The ethnicity of the man is unknown. Video footage shows him breaking the window of a Kelly and Sons' office before throwing some sort of home made bomb inside. These violent protests come after weeks of growing tension due to the so-called gentrification of Toxteth as planning permission was granted to build over local football pitches, seen as a cornerstone of the community, to make way for luxury apartments. Police are asking anyone with information to please come forward. More on this story as it arrives.

Silence.

CHEF. Anybody want a smoke?

BROWNING *reaches for the spliff.* CAROL *pushes her hand away and leaves to the kitchen,* CHEF *follows.*

SHELLY. What were you thinking, Richard, running around like you ain't got nothing to lose. What you gonna do if your job finds out? How we gonna get a mortgage when you're a criminal with no income.

RICHARD. Mortgage? I'm sorry… I… I don't, sorry, I just got carried away.

SHELLY. Carried away? Carried away is eating one too many biscuits. Carried away is driving forty in a thirty zone. Throwing a fucking bomb through a window like you're in *Grand Theft Auto* is terrorism, Richard.

RICHARD. Calm down, Shelly, it wasn't a bomb, they're lying, or exaggerating I don't know, it was a flare. I'm not a terrorist.

SHELLY. No, Richard, you are. What you think 'cause you ain't got a beard you're not a terrorist.

RICHARD. Oh wow, so it's a race thing now?

SHELLY. No it's not, yes it is. What makes you think you can do this shit and get away with it.

RICHARD. I get it, you're angry, let's just / stop for a…

SHELLY. No, let's just nothing. What is wrong with you? You ain't Tocky's saviour, Richard, people don't need you to stick your neck out and do stupid stuff like this.

Is that it? You feel like you need to prove yourself

RICHARD. At least I'm not the fucking sellout…?

CAROL *enters.*

I'm not one of the people that's ruining this place. Can you say the same?

BROWNING. Who ya talking to? I'm sorry, what's he talking about.

SHELLY. Nothing.

Silence in the shop.

RICHARD. Fuck this

He moves towards CAROL.

Sorry, Mrs Hylton.

CAROL. If any of this comes back to here, you broke in and hid in the kitchen yuh understand?

RICHARD. Of course,

SHELLY. Thank you, Mum.

BROWNING. A bomb, Richard?

RICHARD. No, a flare. I know. Look, I grew up here all me life, this is home but I can't even afford to live here. I'm twenty-seven years old work full time but can't afford to move out of my mum's. I used to work in my uncle's corner shop on Parli, losing that place crushed him, you lot probably know him as Mad Jimmy?

CHEF. Mad Jimmy? That's your uncle? I saw him the other day fighting an imaginary cat, I think he was losing the fight too.

RICHARD. Ye thanks, that's Uncle Jimmy.

CAROL. Jimmy was a good man.

RICHARD. You knew him?

CAROL. We went to school together, it's a shame what happened to him. I'm sorry.

RICHARD. Thank you.

SHELLY *and* BROWNING *look at each other in shock.*

BROWNING. Well this is nice, us all together, our little family.

They all look at her.

RICHARD. Mrs Hylton, I've been meaning to ask you something.

BROWNING. Uh-oh.

They all throw their hands up exaggeratedly making FFS sounds and the like, here we go, RICHARD*'s about to ruin the moment of calm.*

RICHARD. I have a friend who's making a film about L8. All about the people that live here and why it's important that Tocky is properly regenerated, not just sold off to the highest bidder. She's looking for local business owners and I thought you would be a great person to ask. Shelly's told me all about how you and Mr Hylton started this place. All we hear now is how tough it is for the locals here, it would be nice to hear about the successful people this place creates too.

BROWNING (*to* SHELLY). Ooohhhh he's good.

CAROL. Oh, I suppose I could… when I have some free time… Rupert.

SHELLY *goes to correct her but* BROWNING *stops her.*

CAROL *is smug, fixes her clothes or something. Comfortable silence.*

RICHARD. I better be on me way, thank you again, Mrs Hylton. Shelly, I'll call you when I get back… we can talk.

SHELLY. Okay.

He moves towards her, he thinks about hugging her maybe, decides not to, he exits.

Thank you, Mum.

CAROL. Mmhmm.

Soft pause and silence in the shop.

SHELLY. Look, Mum, I saw all the letters we been getting…

CAROL. Ohh not now, Shelly, why is it nonstop with you, what do you want from me? I just hid your criminal boyfriend and now you're on me with this shop business again.

SHELLY. We need to talk about it, Mum.

CAROL. Why yuh always want to fight about things. Every day you want to fight about this and about that, I'm tired, Shelly.

SHELLY. I don't want to fight, Mum, I want to talk.

CAROL. Well I don't.

SHELLY. You never do, Mum. You never wanna talk. When I was six and Josh from the year above told me to go back to where I came from, you didn't wanna talk. Always just a smile and a kiss, 'never mind love' you should have fucking copyrighted 'never mind love'. So when I was eighteen and my best friend died, I couldn't talk to you. When I first started uni and couldn't leave my apartment for two months 'cause I was so fucking lost, I didn't want to call you. It's why Browning didn't tell you she was pregnant with Mya until she couldn't hide it. It's why she's too scared to tell you she's gonna quit here when she gets her childcare qualification. It's why Chef doesn't bring you all the amazing food he's been making. It's why he didn't tell you that he could have his food in supermarkets right now but doesn't, because of you. It's why we have never spoken about Dad dying. We have never grieved Dad together, we buried him and then acted like it was business as usual, that's so fucked up, Mum. So that's why I don't understand my 'people', because I want to fucking talk, I just want to be able to talk to you, I want to be able to talk to my people, I want to be able to talk to my mum.

Long silence. SHELLY *cries.*

CAROL *walks over to* SHELLY *and kisses her on her forehead. She calls over* BROWNING. *They all hug.*

CAROL. We can talk about the plans for the shop tomorrow.

SHELLY. Good, because I've been speaking to Kelly and Sons. We couldn't refuse their offer. I've signed all the paperwork, we'll become partners and they're ready to start talking about the redevelopment.

She pulls out some papers.

All the details here. I promise this will be good for us.

An announcement on the radio. They stay frozen in place, shocked, stunned, in a stand-off as it plays out to the auditorium.

TC. Sorry, people. We're cutting that song short. Reports are coming in about a fire in Tocky. We're not sure what has happened yet, the news is coming in as we speak, but early reports state that the football pitches have been attacked and are currently in flames. No news on how this has happened as yet, but we'll keep you posted as soon as we hear more. Stay safe, everyone, please.

A rock comes smashing through the shop window, shattering glass everywhere.

Blackout.

ACT TWO

Scene One

CAROL, SHELLY, BROWNING *and* CHEF *are in the shop.*
CAROL *is peering through a window, while* CHEF *is gathering wood to make a blockade for the door, there isn't much wood… 'cause why would there be, so he is also rather uselessly using some cardboard too. The window has been boarded up.* SHELLY *is swiping through her phone watching videos of the fire at the football pitches.* BROWNING *is frantically trying to call Victor.*

The sound of sirens and the animated voices of people can be heard from outside the shop.

CAROL. What's this supermarket business?

CHEF. Ah, it was just… It's not important, a little thing I was doing but then I couldn't do it.

CAROL. Chef?

CHEF. It was a competition. But I couldn't go to the final, it was when we had a catering job.

CAROL. And Shelly didn't let you go? You should have spoken to me.

CHEF. No I didn't ask her, I wasn't worried about… It just wasn't the right time.

CAROL. But why wouldn't you tell me about it? That's exciting, I would have been excited.

CHEF. I know. Sorry.

CAROL. Sorry. You don't have to stay here you know. If you wanted to go and work somewhere else, or open up your own / shop and…

CHEF. Stop yuh foolishness, Carol, go grab me that cardboard over there and help me put this up.

They share a smile. She rubs his arm.

NEWS REPORTER. Residents of the L8 area in Liverpool are being asked to stay indoors, as rising tensions and clashes between police and protesters have reached boiling point. We now have a confirmed number of forty arrests, whilst twenty-four police officers have been hospitalised, two with life-threatening injuries. A curfew has been placed and large parts of the area cordoned off.

BROWNING (*on the phone*). Victor, what do you want me to do? We're not allowed to leave where we are, police have told everyone to stay indoors. I'm sure you can survive looking after your daughter alone for one night, you can do your work in the morning!

She hangs up the phone. After a moment, there comes a loud bang at the door, repeatedly and violently. They pause what they are doing and look at each other for a moment.

CHEF. We don't want no trouble here. A family business this, we're just trying to keep to ourselves.

The banging persists.

I said I don't want no trouble... ey, listen I have a bat here, by the door. If you come in, I will mash up yar arse.

BROWNING. You ain't got no bat, why did you say that?

CHEF. You have a better idea to scare them off?

SHELLY. This is England, who even has a baseball bat in England?

CHEF. It could be a cricket bat?

Banging again.

RICHARD (*offstage*). Shelly, are you in there?

SHELLY. Oh my gosh, let him in, quick.

SHELLY *rushes over to the door and begins to help* CHEF *release the barricade and let him in.*

In comes RICHARD, *sweaty like he has been running a marathon.*

Thank god.

She hugs RICHARD *tightly. Then remembers they're beefing.*

Have you seen the footy pitches?

RICHARD. I saw the flames as I was halfway down the road.

CAROL. Mek me find out that was you, you likkle Guy Fawkes you, and me ah go beat you black and blue!

RICHARD (*under his breath*). Might accept me if you beat me till I was black at least.

CAROL. Hexcuse you?

RICHARD. No! It wasn't me. It's crazy out there. Police everywhere. Kids are smashing up any building they can get to, they don't care what it is. I don't even recognise half of them.

He notices the smashed, boarded-up window.

Shit! Are you all okay? The fire didn't reach here, did it?

CHEF. We're fine, the rock was probably an accident, everyone loves this shop, nobody wants to harm us.

RICHARD. I saw a video of this group of kids, can't have been more than fifteen, sixteen, pouring something all over the pitches, then someone throws something, few moments later and up it goes, flames everywhere, I ran back as quickly as I could.

SHELLY. Let's get the door blocked again.

CAROL. This shop is a part of the community, nobody wants to trouble us, you heard Chef, the window was probably just an accident.

SHELLY. You really wanna take that risk? Chef, help me board up the door again.

CAROL. Well, it was a part of the community, who knows what it is now you've got your hands on it.

They go to place the barricade back on the door.

BROWNING. So what do we do now?

SHELLY. Just wait I guess. Wait until it dies down.

BROWNING. I can't just stay here all night, I need to get back to Mya and Victor, he's stressing out.

SHELLY. She'll be fine with him.

BROWNING. I want to be with my daughter.

CAROL *goes to comfort* BROWNING. SHELLY *rolls her eyes at this*.

SHELLY (*to* RICHARD). So you still think this is the right way for us to be making a point about the pitches? By burning them down?

RICHARD. No, obviously not, Shelly. I don't know why they did that. We've been organised, but these kids out there now that have come round, they've just taken over, taken it too far.

SHELLY. Just 'cause it's not you and your little hippy, cosmic friends, doesn't mean you're not a part of this. You can't decide how people react. The moment one person sets fire to something, it all becomes fair game.

CHEF. It's true, ain't you ever seen *Do the Right Thing*.

BROWNING. Of course he ain't seen *Do the Right Thing*.

CHEF. Richard, surely you've seen *Do the Right Thing*?

They all look at him for a response… RICHARD shakes his head.

BROWNING. I thought you didn't watch films, Chef.

CHEF. Shhh. (*He acts out the film as appropriate as he tells the story.*) So in *Do The Right Thing*, there's this pizza shop. But it's in a black community. It's where all the black people go, but it's run by this Italian guy called Sal. So Sal has this wall of fame in the pizzeria, but all the famous people on the wall are white, famous white people.

So some of the guys in the area go to the shop and tell Sal that he needs to put some pictures of Black people on the wall. Sal says no, obviously, and kicks them out of the shop. So then they start a boycott, tell everyone not to go to Sal's, 'cause he doesn't care about Black people.

'Sal Bush doesn't care about Black people' (*In the style of K***e We*t's 'George Bush doesn't care about Black people' moment.*)

He laughs to himself, no one else finds it very funny.

Anyway, At the end of the day they all march back in and make the same demand. 'Put some black folk on your wall.' Sal predictably says no again, but this time it all kicks off with his sons and they get in a fight. Police come and surprise surprise, it's the black guys they restrain. But one of them, Radio Raheem, he gets choked out by the police and he dies.

They put him in the police car and drive him off, but everybody know say himdead. Then someone, can't remember who, takes it upon themselves to throw a trash can through the window. That's what Americans call a bin. So this boy throws basically a purple wheelie bin through Sal's window and then all hell breaks loose. They burn the place down. The end. Great film.

RICHARD. What does that have to do with the footy pitches?

BROWNING. In the film they had been on the verge of destruction, of needing a release, and throwing the bin through the window gave the space to let it all out.

CHEF. And it was summer, hot oppressive summer, just like this, that's when it always kicks off.

RICHARD. We attacked Kelly and Sons. Literally the root of the problems here.

SHELLY. They aren't the root of all the problems here, surely you know that?

RICHARD. This isn't my fault, Shelly, you can't actually think this is my fault.

SHELLY. I don't know what I think. All I know is you've become some hooded hero setting fire to shit and now everything is burning.

There is a tense silence for a moment.

BROWNING. I do get it though.

SHELLY. What?

BROWNING. I get it. The protests weren't gonna make any difference, we all know that. So they decided instead of all of this protest going to waste, take it out of their control completely. Burn it down, no use to anyone then. Then everyone can just move on.

SHELLY. What are you talking about, they were gonna dig up the pitches and demolish the changing rooms anyway. They've done the job for them, saved them money even. Don't try and rationalise it, they're just idiots, mindless thugs.

BROWNING. They're not. The developers know that it's not safe now. Whatever they build there, they know it's at risk of attack. If we'll burn down the pitches, we'll do the same to whatever else is there too. Smart.

SHELLY. Can you hear yourself? 'We'? Browning, if they can do that what makes you think they won't burn this place down too?

CAROL. Duppy know who to frighten.

SHELLY. Not now, Mum.

BROWNING. This is always the problem with people like you. People that think they're smarter than the rest of us. You think any extreme reaction is just because people are stupid and don't know how to manage themselves. But they're not, violence is a legitimate response to being ignored. And now you've handed this place over to those same investors, fucking hell, Shelly.

SHELLY. What the fuck is legitimate about this? Why is it so hard for you to accept that some people are out there doing fuckery? I have partnered with people that can help save us. Save us from dying like everything else around here. I've made a sensible business decision, but you're all so clouded by this fake sense of community. Look out there, Browning, look at the glass on the floor, what community do you see here?

BROWNING. Why is it so hard for you to acknowledge that the world doesn't run on neatly made business plans and polite politics? Why is it so hard for you to understand that whether you like it or not, when you talk down on this community to others, they look at you in the same light? You and Mum are both so fucking stubborn that you're tearing this family apart, the same way those developers are tearing this community apart. The same developers you've handed this shop over to without consulting us.

SHELLY. Why would I consult you, Browning, what do you know? I haven't handed anything over, they are partners, with cash, something that you might have noticed, we don't have.

BROWNING. You're so lost.

SHELLY. Okay, cut the bullshit, how about you stop talking to me in poetry and let's put it all out there plain and clear, what is your issue with me?

A loud explosion is heard from outside, it's getting closer.

CHEF. I'm gonna go and clear these up. Richard, come help me with the dishes.

RICHARD. Yes please.

He nods in agreement, or grunts yes. They go to the kitchen sharpish.

BROWNING. Fine. I think you're a snob.

SHELLY. I think you're naive. Your turn.

CAROL. Girls, stop this foolishness.

BROWNING. No, Mum, it's fine.

> CAROL *goes to a table and picks up the documents*
> SHELLY *was brandishing about the deal, she begins to read*
> *them.*

I think you have a superiority complex.

SHELLY. I think you never grew up and you still think you're the baby.

BROWNING. I think you think you're too good for Liverpool.

SHELLY. I think you're jealous of me.

BROWNING. I think you're delusional.

SHELLY. I think you don't know a thing about the real world.

BROWNING. I think you think you're better than us.

SHELLY. I think you're too scared to live your own life.

BROWNING. I think you're a brat.

SHELLY. I think you lack ambition.

BROWNING. I think you're selfish.

SHELLY. I think you're irresponsible.

BROWNING. I think you're arrogant.

SHELLY. I think you're impulsive.

BROWNING. I think you're self-absorbed.

SHELLY. I think you're crude.

BROWNING. I think you're fake.

SHELLY. I think you're lazy.

BROWNING. I think you're lonely.

SHELLY. I think you're scared.

BROWNING. You ran away from us when Dad died.

SHELLY. You wasted your life having Mya so young.

BROWNING. You're a cunt.

Beat.

SHELLY. You don't know me.

BROWNING. You don't want to know me.

SHELLY. You don't see me.

BROWNING. You're ashamed of me.

SHELLY. I think you and Mum don't like me.

They hold whatever this space is. Nothing is resolved, nothing feels better. They can hold this in silence for as long as they need to.

CAROL. This agreement… Shelly. And you've signed this?

SHELLY.…

CAROL. Well you can call them, you can't sign this without me, we are joint owners, I have to sign it.

SHELLY. You did. You signed it, the agreement I said was for catering…

BROWNING goes over to CAROL with pace and takes the agreement from her. She scrambles to get a lighter and repeatedly tries to light it, but it's not working.

Browning. They have a copy of the agreement. They have digital copies, what do you think burning the agreement is going to do.

BROWNING. Oh shut up, always so fucking clever.

SHELLY. Gimme the lighter, Browning.

BROWNING. No.

She attempts to light it, but she struggles, flicking it over and over.

Fuck's sake.

SHELLY. Want some help?

BROWNING. Shut up! You just shut up.

With this, it flicks on and lights the paper, it starts burning.

Ha, haha, see, I did it, it's lit.

SHELLY. What you gonna do now?

BROWNING *realises the burning paper is getting closer and closer to her hand.*

BROWNING. Shit, shit, shit!

She's looking around to see what she should do with it. She blows on it, stupid. They all start panicking now, moving closer and further away from BROWNING *and the fire.*

SHELLY. Throw it in the sink in the kitchen?

CAROL. No, don't throw it in there, you eejit, that's where Chef pours the oil.

BROWNING. What should I do with it then?

SHELLY. I don't know, this was your bright idea!

CAROL. Put it in the bin.

BROWNING *throws it in the bin. It immediately lights up even stronger and bigger, they all scream.*

BROWNING. Is it meant to do that?

The fire alarm starts going off. They are panicking, fanning at the fire. CHEF *comes bursting into the room with* RICHARD *behind him. He is holding a fire extinguisher, and he puts the fire out, hurrah. They all slump down and sit across the space.* CHEF *lights another spliff. He passes it to* CAROL.

CAROL. Jesus.

Beat.

Your dad would be sick if he could see what is happening right now.

When your dad first reach England, he was in London first you know.

Him and his mother did down there for the first couple of years, but they never get along with London much. His mum had a friend who had gone straight to Liverpool and said she loved it, so without knowing anything else, she moved with your dad up here.

He always said the first thing he noticed was the air. The air felt fresher, not like home, but closer to it.

Then he got older, he realised that the streets of Liverpool weren't paved in gold either. School was tough for him, but he built himself a little community, here. And it grew, and grew, and the people in Liverpool looked out for him, cared for each other in a way that they never had in London. The whole community, all kinda people and all kinda races... scousers first isn't it. He used to play on those very same football pitches next door. Your dad loved this city. And not just because of the water, but because of the people. When he said he wanted to open this shop I said no, I never wanted to be a businesswoman, I was a good nurse. But when that man get an idea, there's no changing him.

If he could see the three of us right now, falling apart over the thing that brought him love, and family, and community. He would be sick.

I always knew the world could turn on us, but I never thought we would turn on each other.

BROWNING. Did either of you even think about how it felt for me that Dad left the shop to you two and not me?

Beat.

SHELLY *goes towards her sister to comfort her. Before she reaches her –*

It's fine.

SHELLY. Maybe he didn't want you to be weighed down by this place like us.

BROWNING. And maybe he thought it would bring you two together, not tear you apart.

Another beat.

CAROL. I did grieve your dad.

SHELLY. It's okay, Mum, there's a lot going on tonight, you don't have / to now

CAROL. / I didn't know how to grieve in front of you, but I did grieve. For a long time. I miss your father very much. I will continue to miss him for the rest of my life. He told me he was going to leave the shop to you as well, Shelly, before he died. Said that it would be too much for just me, that I needed the help. Cheek of the man. Good enough to nurse him on his deathbed but can't sell a patty. I didn't want you to have to take on the burden, Shell, you shouldn't have to. I thought I could do it alone, I wanted him to know, or to feel, wherever his spirit landed, that I could do it alone.

I won't feel guilty for trying to be strong for you both.

BROWNING. You've always been strong enough for us, Mum, sometimes too strong. We're not babies any more.

CAROL. You think there will ever be a day when Mya isn't your baby? She will always be your baby, you can't help it.

BROWNING. I get it, but adults still need parents too. Just different kinds of parents, and if you always see us as your babies, you'll deny us the mum we need, as adults.

Beat.

I think me and Victor are going to break up. I know you can probably see it anyway, but you're pretending you can't. That's why I came here tonight, with my bags. I left him and Mya at home and I came here, because I need my mum, and this shop, and my sister, and my dad I guess, I came here because where the fuck else could I go.

They pause and take note of that for a moment, acknowledging in silence, in their own ways.

CAROL. I'm so sorry, Browning.

SHELLY. We're here.

Beat.

I just wanted to make Dad proud.

CAROL. I think I did too.

BROWNING. We all did. But we should just be proud of ourselves, shouldn't we.

SHELLY. I don't want to forget his face. I want to remember him.

CAROL. You will never forget his face, Shelly

SHELLY. No I know, I know I won't. But I mean like vivid memories. Not memories that you have to question whether it's really yours or just a story you heard. I used to be able to feel him around me when I thought of him. I don't get that any more.

CAROL. Sometimes when I really miss him, I play music that he loved, and I dance, by myself, but I feel him with me, just how you said. I understand.

Lord Jesus, you must think your mother tun fool isn't it?

SHELLY. No. Not at all. Thank you, Mum.

CAROL *cups* SHELLY*'s face.*

CAROL. Just look in the mirror. Or look at your sister. Or look at this shop, and the people that come in here because he made them feel like this place was home when outside there didn't. You'll never forget him, I won't let you, I promise you that.

Beat.

I'm sorry, to both of you.

Now, is there something you two would like to say to each other?

SHELLY *and* BROWNING. Sorry.

CAROL. Try again.

BROWNING. I love you, Shelly. You're fucking annoying, but I love you. And I know how much you love me. I was being mean.

SHELLY. I was being mean too. I think maybe actually I am a bit jealous of you. And how much people love you, and how you can talk to anyone about anything. How people always light up when you enter the room. I admire you.

BROWNING. Say again.

SHELLY. No!

They embrace each other. It's loving and raw and painful, but necessary.

SHELLY *begins to sing, gently: 'Down by the River' by Morgan Heritage.*

CAROL. Shelly…

SHELLY *continues to sing as* RICHARD *and* CHEF *come in. They join in the song (when theatrically appropriate and not jarring). As they do,* SHELLY *dances with her mum, joyous. a slow embraced dance.* CHEF *and* RICHARD *continue singing the song as they do.*

The song ends.

SHELLY. Mum.

CAROL. Yes, baby.

SHELLY. I'll call the investors in the morning and tell them it's off. I'll find a way out, tell them I forged your signature.

CAROL. Never mind, love… I mean, yes, it's really bad, this is really bad, but no matter what happens, we'll work through it together from now on, business partner.

She looks at BROWNING.

Partners.

BROWNING. No more fraud and shit? That's proper illegal you know.

SHELLY. Promise.

BROWNING. No more hiding things?

CAROL. Promise.

The three of them embrace each other. CHEF *and* RICHARD *look at each other, they hug too.*

Come, Browning, let's go pick up Mya, we can all walk together, the shop will be fine without us. Then we can all go home together, watch a movie or something.

SHELLY. I'm not watching one of those old dramatic Jamaican movies though.

CAROL. And I'm not watching *Sex ina di City* or no foolishness like that.

(*To* RICHARD *and* CHEF.) Chef, Richard, you coming?

CHEF *and* RICHARD *look at each other in disbelief, is she really asking us?*

RICHARD (*mumbled responses together*). Yeah yeah, sure thing, okay, sure.

BROWNING. I'm just gonna get Mya's tablet from the back, I'll catch up with you in a sec.

They all go to leave. CAROL *turns to* CHEF *and gives him a kiss on the cheek, the girls are grossed out.* CAROL, CHEF *and* SHELLY *exit.*

RICHARD. I'll wait with you.

BROWNING. You're okay, superman, you won't get that invite from Mum twice, go on before they leave you.

RICHARD. You're not gonna try and burn the place down again are ya?

BROWNING. Maybe.

RICHARD. Let me know if you need any tips next time.

He leaves, leaving BROWNING *alone. She waits to see that they are gone. she goes behind the counter and pulls out one of the dishes* CHEF *has been working on. She takes a bite, savours it.*

BROWNING. Just a tiny bit more sugar.

She smiles and sprinkles a little sugar on the dish.

Perfect

Blackout.

End.

A Nick Hern Book

Takeaway first published in Great Britain as a paperback original in 2025 by Nick Hern Books Limited, The Glasshouse, 49a Goldhawk Road, London W12 8QP in association with Liverpool Everyman & Playhouse Theatres.

Takeaway copyright © 2025 Nathan Powell

Nathan Powell has asserted his right to be identified as the author of this work

Cover design by Kerry Spicer

Designed and typeset by Nick Hern Books, London
Printed in Great Britain by Mimeo Ltd, Huntingdon, Cambridgeshire PE29 6XX

A CIP catalogue record for this book is available from the British Library

ISBN 978 1 83904 468 7

www.nickhernbooks.co.uk/environmental-policy

Nick Hern Books' authorised representative in the EU is
Easy Access System Europe – Mustamäe tee 50, 10621 Tallinn, Estonia
email gpsr.requests@easproject.com

www.nickhernbooks.co.uk

@nickhernbooks